Changes on Earth

by Cassandra Jenkins

What are Earth's layers?

Earth's Layers

Earth is divided into three layers. The **crust** is the outer layer of Earth. It is made up of different kinds of rock. The thickness of the crust is different in different places. The crust is about 37 kilometers (23 miles) thick under the continents. Compare Earth to a peach. The crust would be the skin of the peach.

The **mantle** is below the crust. It is made up of very hot rocks. It can flow like thick toothpaste.

The **core** is the innermost layer of Earth. It is made up of metal. The core is so hot that it could melt. But it is packed tightly together and stays mostly solid. Its outer part is a very hot liquid.

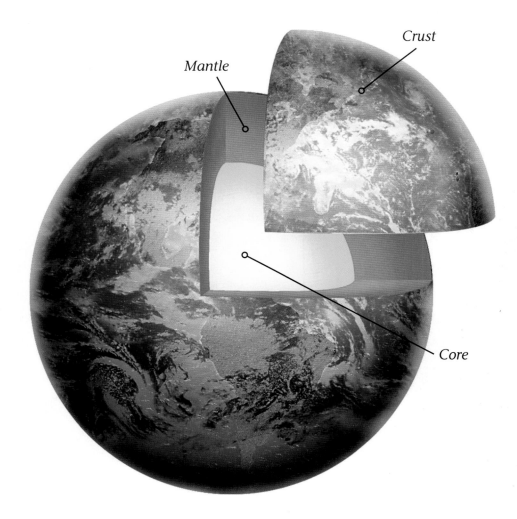

Crust

Mantle

Core

Shapes on Earth's Surface

A **landform** is a solid feature on Earth's crust. Mountains, hills, and valleys, are landforms. Other features include bodies of water. There are many different types of landforms on Earth.

Forces shape these landforms. Moving water is a strong force. Rivers can act as saws. Sand and pebbles in the water slowly cut through rock. Flooding rivers leave silt, sand, and pebbles on their banks. These things help form valleys.

Glacier

Valley

Plateau

Ocean

Coast

Do you recognize these landforms?

A glacier is a moving body of ice. It slowly moves downhill. A volcano is an opening in Earth's crust. Hot, melted rock is forced through it. Some mountains form when pieces of rock are pushed along cracks in Earth's crust. A lake forms when water flows slowly enough to fill up an area.

Volcano   Mountain   Lake   River   Hill   Plain

This picture shows a mountain, a kind of landform, and a lake.

What are volcanoes and earthquakes?

How Do Volcanoes Form?

Volcanoes start in the mantle. This is where **magma** forms. Magma is hot, partly melted rock that is under pressure from gases it contains. This pressure forces it up through Earth's crust. The hot material erupts through an opening in a volcano.

Lava is the material that erupts from a volcano. Lava has ash, cinders, and hot rock in it. As lava cools, it becomes new crust.

This lava was once magma inside Earth.

Volcanoes

Magma collects in large pockets. These pockets are called magma chambers. As magma leaves a chamber, it moves up a tunnel or vent. Sometimes magma escapes and erupts from a side vent. But most magma erupts through a central vent. It erupts through a bowl-shaped crater at the top of the volcano.

Crater

Central vent

Side vent

Side vent

Magma chamber

Earthquakes

Parts of Earth's crust can shift suddenly. This causes the ground to vibrate. This shaking is called an earthquake. Most earthquakes begin along a fault. A fault is a large crack in Earth's crust.

Earthquake vibrations move as waves through Earth. They also move up and down. The waves can cause cracks. They can pile up rubble in areas around the parts of the crust that moved.

Earthquake Damage

How much earthquake damage occurs depends on how long the crust shakes. It also depends on how close the earthquake is to the surface. Earthquakes can happen very close to a city. This causes a lot of damage to buildings, bridges, pipes, and roads.

An earthquake can cause landslides. Landslides are downhill movements of rocks and earth. Landslides can happen on the land or the ocean floor. Landslides underwater can cause huge waves. Landslides on the land can bury large areas.

Earthquakes can cause damage in cities and in nature.

What are weathering and erosion?

Weathering

Landforms are always changing. This happens when rocks in landforms break apart. **Weathering** is any action that breaks rocks into smaller pieces.

Weathering goes on all the time. It causes changes over time. Some changes might take a year. Others could take hundreds of years.

Plants can cause weathering. Their roots grow into rocks. As the roots grow, they break apart rocks.

Water mixed with decayed material in soil can also cause weathering. This water changes the minerals in the rock. The rock grows weak and starts to break apart. Water can also seep in and freeze in the cracks of a rock. Then the water expands. Ice pushes against the rock and breaks it apart over time.

Ice changes rocks in a different way. Glaciers are huge bodies of ice. Rocks and ice scrape against the ground as a glacier moves. This makes valleys wide and smooth. Rocks of all sizes drop to the ground when the glacier melts. These rocks and soil line the edges where the glacier used to be.

Boulder

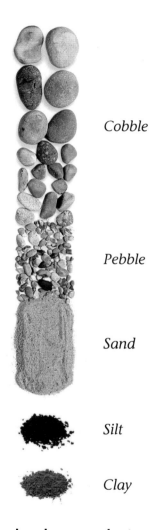

Cobble

Pebble

Sand

Silt

Clay

Look at how weathering has broken down this boulder into smaller and smaller pieces.

Erosion

Sometimes weathered materials are picked up and carried away. The movement of weathered materials is called **erosion.** Glaciers, gravity, wind, and water can cause erosion.

Water erosion is the most common form. Rivers move bits of rock. During floods, mud and sand flow over a river's banks. Rainwater washes soil away from hills.

Erosion can make new islands. Rivers carry rocks and soil to the ocean. They build up over time into islands. Then wind and waves change their shape.

In dry places such as deserts, wind often causes erosion. Wind can pick up dry sand and soil. It blows them to other places since there aren't many plants to hold them down. The particles bump into rocks and cause small grains to break off. Slowly the rocks change.

Living things can cause erosion. Some squirrels tunnel through soil. Worms can mix and carry soil to new places. Groups of ants move soil to make nests. When an animal tunnels, it allows water and air into the ground. Then the air and water continue the erosion.

Erosion caused the hole in this cliff.

Gravity causes erosion by pulling rocks downhill. This material moves slowly unless the slope is steep. Weathered material moves very quickly on steep slopes! The movement of wet soil is called a mudflow. When rocks slide quickly down a hill, it is called a rockslide.

This hillside eroded. The side of the hill slumped down.

Glossary

core   the innermost layer of Earth

crust   the outer layer of Earth

erosion   the movement of weathered material

landform   a solid feature formed on Earth's crust

lava   molten rock that erupts from a volcano

magma   hot, partly melted rock that is under pressure

mantle   the part of Earth just beneath the crust

weathering   any action that breaks rocks into smaller pieces